Cattle Console Him

Cattle Console Him

Chris Preddle

WAYWISER

First published in 2010 by

THE WAYWISER PRESS

Bench House, 82 London Road, Chipping Norton, Oxon OX7 5FN, UK
P.O. Box 6205, Baltimore, MD 21206, USA
http://waywiser-press.com

Editor-in-Chief
Philip Hoy

Senior American Editor
Joseph Harrison

Associate Editors
Clive Watkins   Greg Williamson

Cover image: Dubuffet, Jean (1901-1985): *The Cow with the Subtile Nose*,
from the 'Cows, Grass, Foliage' series, 1954. New York, Museum of Modern Art
(MoMA). Oil and enamel on canvas, 35 x 45 3/4' (88.9 x 116.1 cm).
Benjamin Scharps and David Scharps Fund. 288.1956© 2010.
Digital image, The Museum of Modern Art, New York/Scala, Florence.

Copyright © Chris Preddle, 2010

The right of Chris Preddle to be identified as the author of this work
has been asserted by him in accordance with the
Copyright, Designs and Patents Act of 1988.

All rights reserved

A CIP catalogue record for this book is available from the British Library

ISBN 978-1-904130-41-3

Printed and bound by
Cromwell Press Group, Trowbridge, Wiltshire BA14 0XB

for Jacqui

Acknowledgements

'Variations on Sappho 95' first appeared in *Stand* (8, 2, no.186, 2008).

Other poems have appeared in *Anon*, *Envoi*, *Orbis*, *PN Review*, *Poetry Review*, *The Rialto*, *Scintilla*, *The Shop*, *Smiths Knoll*, and *The Yellow Nib*, and on the websites of *Agenda* and the Robert McLellan Poetry Award.

Contents

I

Water Sonnets	13
King Socrates	16
The Tower	21
The Bench	22
On Chris	23
The Desk	28
Porteous	29
Bohemia	30
Not Catullus	31
Geodesy	33
The Arrowloop	34
What the Streetlamp Said	35
Black	36
Earthmover	37
Tank	38
Ruin	39
Issues Road	40

II

Variations on Sappho 95	45

III

First Letter to Ed	65
Second Letter to Ed	67
Third Letter to Ed	69
The Left Arm	70
Your Body Undressed	71
In Sicyon	72

Contents

Narcissus Poeticus 73
Grass 74
Cattle Console Him 75
These Cattle 77
Reaching Chios 78
Groundsel 79
For a Wedding 80

IV

Holme 83

A Note about the Author 95

I

Water Sonnets

1 A Body of Water

The old Turkish road that we walked to Lithi bay
was so bouldery it would've unhorsed a bey
from his chestnut or bay.

That beach in Greece, both stony and sandy,
was where I longed like a song for you, Danny for Sandy,
as the waves slid up and down like glissandi.

Rupert our guide was asleep in a cool place, Brer Rupert.
Margaret your chaperone left us, whom the dragon ate, Saint Margaret.

Behind my back, alas, you addressed
the business of getting undressed
as the waves came up in a wavy line, their long rank not dressed.

We entered the Greek sea,
a body of water curved to your own body, like a C.
We swam further than anyone could see.

Water Sonnets

2 Waterwife

You liked to swim when the windsurfers' wind,
the *ora* of Lake Garda
uncombed your hair like surf unwound
from the lake's breakers and combers.

Waterwife, between wind and water, come back. I guard you,
beached myself. The waves are as high
as our coom-
ceiled attic, my ivory attic high and dry.

From my uttermost attic I bend over the sill
like an ingrown nail, and look for you, lakelady, far-off in the swim
of things, a skelf
of your swimming self.
Even the attic with its *sprezzatura*, its airs in the swarm of air
must surf the wind like a boardsail.

Water Sonnets

3 The Sink

This ruin is the Baths of Cleopatra, so said
our Greekling guide. If Cleo patronised

such a minor
Roman municipal facility on the coast of Asia Minor,

I'm the Emperor Theodore. Its stones sank
as the sea level rose. We never thought to have sunk

so low. Lo, below your swimming form
the ruin looms, said our cicerone, like a Platonic form.

Indeed. Whatever underlies
our Christian civilisation and the lays and lies

of East Rome, however the migrants and Muhammedans
(as the Emperor says) have hemmed us in,

teach me, Jacqueline, to swim, not sink,
above this sunken rectangle which waits like an open sink.

King Socrates

1

Brother armarius,
lend me a certain book from your armary,

not a missal or book of hours
by which the assurances of Christ have been made ours,

no Rule (*Benedictus qui venit*)
for living in common since all is vanity,

no life of a saint
to whose high-sky certitudes I should make an assent,

lend me the book that ascertains
human certainties,

from which I may divine myself, certes,
The Prognostications of King Socrates.

2

The frontispiece of this book of fate (the Bodleian's
MS Ashmole 304, folio 31 verso),
drawn by Matthew Paris of St Albans,
reverses

all we expect: 'King' Socrates, dubious and d-d-dunce-
like, writes at a throne of a desk; Plato,
down-in-the-mouth at his back, wags a finger and d-d-dances
with exasperation. They're Mickey and Pluto.

This reconstructed image of instruction on a postcard
deconstructed the certainties of Derrida,
however we may deride *The Post Card*
for its psychoanalyticosexual problematizing of the pedagogic power
    structure, deda-deda.

Sarcastic Plato has divined that certainty accretes
more and more to this *sacerdos* of secrets, this Christ of curiosity.

King Socrates

3

Petitioner, turn the volvelle
while 'sodenly thynkyng on the question':
volve and revolve

in your mind the foreknowledge you are requesting
while you turn like a turntable
my wheel-within-a-wheel which answers your inquisiting

with a number. Turn to a table. Turn to a table.
Turn to a new 'sphere'
of plants or creatures or cities. How far you've come. Like a laid table

a city is drawn on my page. Its king, though false as Pharaoh,
assures you what will evolve.
Do not expect to see that it's fair or what it's for.

4

Brother mathematicus, fie,
find me a certainty to defy

the unkind acts of human- and godkind. Sex in the cloister
is no more loving than a clyster,

the volvelle
turns down like a nun my wish to unveil a vulva.

If certainty is merely a formula
for calculating the next perfect number, let me be famulus familiar

to her who cared all winter
for what had found a certain refuge inside her window,

the lacewing
to which she gave solace, which she took under her wing.

King Socrates

5

As diagonals
drawn from angle to angle of a regular pentagon
always intersect
in the Divine Proportion, Leonardo's Golden Section,

fie, Jacqueline, fie,
beautiful things in this ratio of phi for Phidias
seem to outnumber
even beauties of your form and self I'd thought without number.

No. Because
those numbers-in-relation
are our opposites, exact, abstract, replicative, causeless,

I, human-
in-relation, now relate
how in numbers I number your beauties for their humanness.

The Tower

No matter how often the TV replayed
the plane igniting the tower, no matter how many
fell like any sky-
borne plague of Egypt from the disobedient East,

the watchers in a kafenion in the Mani –
Katastrophí, katastrophí! – a Greek chorus, replied
in the answering strophe, 'You in the West
have brought it on yourselves. It's gone home, Yankees.'

Volta. *Káno vólta,* I take a turn
round the top of this afflicted tower
we rent for a season. About turn. I watch like a Maniot
for all that I've brought on
myself, no matter how often I tour (about tour)
these battelments distrest. No matter.

The Bench

for Chris

Air: The Dawning of the Day

Your postcard's come from Dublin: Oscar as if in a drawingroom,
declined on oscular fur on a sofa in oscarybosky gloom,
a chiaroscaroscuro carpet-moth. (My fairy fey,
you were Paris fair and passing fair at the dawning of your day.)

'This louche guy suited you, I thought' – though it could be 'lâche'
    or 'lush',
your writing's lax – 'relaxed slipshod in slippers of velvet plush.'
Alas, your sight's half lost; he sits in slip-on pumps, I'd say,
glossed to be seen on the social scene in the noontime of his day.

The Writers Museum's closed today, but its dead are on their feet
and follow you, as conclusions follow, along O'Connell Street,
these righteous, wry and gone-awry; with a cane you feel your way
from kerb to kerb, the crowds uncurbed in the postnoon of the day.

And purblind Joyce is following, raised Triestine from tristesse –
proscribed ('Hence, vain deluding Joyce'), he inscribed a conclud-
    ing Yes –
and Yeats, released from Ballylee; you're tired but would essay
O'Connell Bridge like a footsore ridge in the evening of your day.

With creep and crepitus you aspire towards the canalside statue
of Kavanagh declined on a bench, the bench where once he sat you,
his sofa at dusk, creposcarcrepuscular. Now he's aspired away
and declines conclusions or any clues in the nighttime of your day.

On Chris

1

Chris on a kickstool, with a crick
in his neck, reaches for *The Poems & Letters of Andrew Marvell*
as if for a higher knowledge. Marvell himself
paces the room like his own metre; his boots creak.

The poet won't take a fixed position
on Cromwell or anything else, but ranges Chris's shelves
leafing and leaving volumes with a continual removal.
The kickstool creaks; a poet is an imposition.

Marvell, if you or I is merely a shifting disposition,
a mood for a poem, a constant dispossession
of whatever we were, I'm nothing on a kickstool.

Kickstool, stalk I stand on highly exalted,
we are not the world tree after all but an axletree
of nothing. We're kickstool and carcass.

On Chris

2

Chris on a walkingstick, not much of an alpenstock,
has climbed Black Hill, with the help
of Keira the uncynical dog. His mood is cynical.
This soggy summit, not much of an Alp, is now their sum of things.

Peatbogs, I may be as well sucked in,
suckled to death. I have come by hobble and hirple
to your black bogwater, sink one sink all,
the melancholy humour of things.

He descends Black Hill. A field trip from Holme School
came up, children sanguine, choleric or ever-so-cool,
descendants of those he would gladly suffer.

Such men and women, Keira thought, such Helens
to their lovers, such slender saplings, in the words of Sappho,
who lives nearby – we meet her in the lanes.

On Chris

3

Chris on the rec, halt and lame, Chris who's a wreck
himself (as he says), contemplates an Ireland
of the mind, with Ciara the saintly dog, Kiera
the contemplative, nunlike, none like her.

This playing field, a dog's walk, is my townland
of all the writers, rioters and wrongs of Ireland. A cloud wrack
on Holme Moss is the Otherworld. Its gentle Sidhe
were good to me. And she, ah, none like she.

He circled the rec. But I do not care
to be so much determined by the there and then
and here and now. I would be other than.

And Ceara the canonised won't be a form
canonical. They shall not spell her. *Verbum*
Ciora *factum est*, she barks, the word's made Keera.

On Chris

4

Chris on the Wake. Today's listen is, gaudeamus earwigtour,
colossical texticle, sexhindered
ineternity wait purges, gladsome and gadsome, it wag
all lusive, spun of nups and unps, all's kindred.

Curse of, this razes the quest, Ion, of the sylph,
who is selfia, what am she, and of
the hole of it, not half, dissolfed, not soulfish, not I, sell flesh.
    Elusieve.
Sorrowmost I am to have to have come to the end of.

However, Corydon ever insinuates,
like an air of his flute, his sylvan self
round Phyllida. 'A separate self is a slough

to be left behind. The spirit extenuates
the body. Your body is apple flesh.' And it seems,
apple-lonely Phyllida feels the same, selfsame.

On Chris

5

Chris on a white stick, Chris who's a crock
(he says it himself) in a hi-vis yellow
jacket, has climbed Meal Hill
with *kirA* the godheaded dog the shape of her own cartouche.

Some day O let him be buried in a shaft or crack
of this very hill or pyramid, as this valley
is our Valley of the Kings. He descends Meal Hill
with *kirA* the dogheaded god; they go by touch.

At the bottom a line of children was going back
to Holme School ('in a crocodile, please!'),
descendants of those he used to teach.

These are the children of Krokodilon Polis,
who have visited their crocodile god. On his back
there was yellow gold and a jewel like a saffron crocus.

The Desk

for Jacob

Sit at this desk
whose grain crackles, creaks
and expects you now, a century since it grew big by the Lune,
as young Johann Sebastian the very first time in Lüneburg
sat in the Johanniskirche
at the organ desk.

Porteous

for Katrina

Looking up something else I've found your name
defined in the *OED*. A porteous
was the breviary of the medieval church, the daily office
it chose to ordain

for the ordained. Once I would make use of
Thomas's *Imitation* like that. 'For there is no man
without his faults,' said the Penguin book, 'none without his
    burden.'
Such words, I thought, were a poet's,

though he wrote in the name of Christ pegged out
like his own windingsheet. There's no such book
I would resort to now, but abandon all

I've slept on like pillows for the intellect. In doubt
let's turn as you turn back
to the material boats, beach and sea at Beadnell.

Bohemia

for Ken Bell

You've found this lost edition
Derek had searched for all his life,
The Winter's Tale with its errors, leaf
by human leaf,
cancelled,
rescued like Leontes from perdition
by a secondhand bookseller and his Bohemian love,
just where Derek used to live;

though you've completed his Shakespeare at secondhand,
keep on, Ken, go as far
as Paris or Bohemia, go to bookstalls, fairs
and festivals, consider your search, not cancelled,
consoled,
take him to book-cellars and backrooms, visit Shakespeare and Co.

Not Catullus

for Ken Walker

1

This ruined villa never belonged to Catullus,
you'll be disappointed to learn. These five acres of overbearing
    masonry,
of arches, porches and porticos (the scholars tell us),

this belvedere the height of a dozen Romans
were beyond your poet's pocket, their sumptuary insolence
too much even for him. Though they stand on the heights of
    Sirmione,

his darling eye of islands and peninsulas,
a promontory, as he might have put it, poking into the bottom
of Lake Garda like Silenus' penis,

this was not the homestead that he came skippingly home to
from his labours in Bithynia, not where he wrote of the crisis
with Lesbia. The owner of this pile with a lake for a moat

was a cross between Caesar, Pompey or Crassus, and Croesus;
the barge he sat in, like a bum-burnished throne,
burned up the water on his cruises.

Not Cartullus

2

We've made it home to the world's-end Britons, their world-with-
    out-end north,
and it's you passing our front gate, six foot six
in flip-flops, bearing down on the mailbox. Yourself, none other,

would fit that generous villa, not merely for an excess
of inches – you who travel continents
from school to school with stories from the Tiber, Euphrates and Oxus,

in Roman dress, a senator in a schoolroom; you who happily consent,
for one who is dying, to be her singer of tales,
reading aloud to her all the novels of Jane Austen.

Geodesy

St Helena, 1910. Harriet is on horseback
side-saddle, decorative, and sitting off-centre
like the island itself off-centre in the South Atlantic.

Horse and Harriet are each girt with a secret cincture,
a girth or undergirdle. An ever-
fixèd mark, they decline to walk, let alone canter.

The foldlines of her pleated skirt, in a half-
circle like a protractor, lengthen and with Puck's virtue
put themselves like a girdle round the earth.

So Harriet on her high horse, which never curvets
or pirouettes, which bears her like a settee soft and saddleback,
is the centre of the world's geodetic curves.

The Arrowloop

The archer at an embrasure
had an outlook like ours here at the back, narrow
between our bathroom extension that intersects
the sky like a bastion, and next door's massy gable-end
at a salient angle. I see no more
than Tim's hollytrees that march
like a curtainwall over his meadow, the holegns and hollins
that gave their name to this vill of Holne
in *Domesday*. This is as much
as I see when I write, this mere
locality, this little Walden Pond
on which we do as we can, we skater insects.
His small view compels the archer at an arrow-
loop as he warms his hands at a brazier.

What the Streetlamp Said

The high streetlamp, on its hind legs
like a stick-insect, shines on with a blackleg's

high obstinacy, between and through our lined
bedroom curtains. I've tried to blinker or blind

its light by shooting at it with a catapult,
climbing its firemen's pole with an axe, and pelting

its head-in-the-clouds with old shirts, breeches
and undershorts. I failed to reach it.

I'm reminded of the shunting yards floodlit
in Hornsey, where I lived for ten years in a flatlet

as high as this lamppost. Under its high light
I analyse the pros and cons, the low- and highlights

of that London period. The lamp, though its brain is sodium,
shakes its orange head. It's not so dumb,

and forces the point of the present through the curtain
like a rapier through the arras, just to make certain.

Black

The quartet lift their fiddlebows
like eyebrows, and pause. Dressed in matt black,
four just men, they commence their labours

with Haydn and Mozart, then ply the baleful Bartok
with its high anxieties. As we leave
I think, 'As if more were needed!' We're late back

at Holme, where the moors with one resolve
sit down like black cattle hearing thunder in the index.
I must fetch in coal, and dig with a tiny shovel

into the bunker. The coals, manufactured hexa-
hedrons and ellipsoids of revolution,
revolve and roll away like disaffected eggs

that I dropped as a child in a film-noir version
of an egg-and-spoon race. They will not cohere,
the blackguards. On Black Hill the television

transmitter mast we can see from here
sticks up like a lifted bow. The quartet pause, with elbows
poised; there's something I still need to hear.

Earthmover

Richard in his field drives a hired loader
between a dumptruck and his spoil-
heap, and digs away at the established order

we've known from our window, that bank of earth and ordure.
Its topsoil,
or whatever he's driving at with the tyre loader,

is colonised by grasses, foxgloves, rhodo-
dendrons and a Chinese parasol-
tree happy to dig in, their self-established order

like a peace. He has felled a forest of cedar
sweeter than oil –
he's having a field-day as he drives the tireless loader,

Gilgamesh in a Lada.
I stretched in the medicinal milfoil
and hoped – but he digs away. He has disestablished the order

of us who sat like Buddha
under his banyan with its trunks in a coil and moil.
Richard, in the field of words they derive the tiring loader

from Old English *lād*: a leading, a road or
journey, a carrying. By toil
you hope to dig away the established disorder.

Follow-the-loader, follow-the-leader,
sing not here the pastourelle.
Richard in his field contrives the tired loader,
the heap is dug away, he has re-established order.

Tank

In this year not of our election,
as Sarah clip-clops by on a round horse
with a girth like our oil tank,

the Elected One
himself came by at a clip, hoping we'd endorse
his riding into the sunrise on a tank.

Ruin

Smurry smoory smeary rain
is blowing down from Holme Moss and its moor
on hawthorn, rowan

and holly or holme, on sheepwalks, on cattle red and roan,
on us. Jacqui and Chris, Mary
and Ken, we bend against the windbent rain,

which comes at us and our roofs, shutters and rones
in combative waves like an army.
We live (we live well) in the policy and reign

of an emperor (Imp.) of the west, who runs
like a rain gutter around the limits of things, whose humour
affects us (imp!) like a murrain.

He arraigned (aroint thee) and overran
Holme and Babylonia and the Country of the Living. Errant Sumer
he made a ruin.

Issues Road

'No, no,' said Ken, 'Constantine the Great
is altogether different
from George W Bush,
though even then the Brits in decline and fall
acclaimed Constantine's
election of power as if he'd been duly elected.'

Ken and Mary and Jacqui and I had elected
to walk Issues Road, that ungrate-
ful stony track, as Constantine
the Punitive, the Indifferent,
would march to the Eastern wastes. It was the fall.
As far as the moor there's not a tree or bush.

This track, I thought, though it has no burning bush,
is where a penitent self-elected
might fall
to his Christian knees and crawl, where the ingrate
god, no different
from an emperor, might punish the guilt we're constant in.

'No, no,' said Ken, 'Constantine
the Groat and the Texan bush-
president, though indeed the East was insufficiently deferent
to divinely elected' –
I missed the rest, the wind so great
that issues from Issue Clough like a waterfall.

This track, like a civilization in its rise and fall,
aspires to Issue Edge. Constantin-
ople aspired, his great
City. The aspiring penitent, with a branch of a thornbush
to beat himself, has elected
to believe that he and the emperor-god are altogether different.

Issues Road

Ken and Mary and Jacqui and I, indifferent
to those aspirations, rose and fell with the rise and fall
of the track we've elected.
We saw prisoners of Constantine
bush-
whacked to the ground, and heard their leg-irons grate.

'Yes, different – however great
the numbers they elected to the dead – bushy-tailed Constantine
and (the fall of the track) the constantly unconscionable Bush.'

II

Variations on Sappho 95

Sappho fragment 95

Hermes himself came in. I said,
'My lord, by the blessed goddess it's true,
I get no pleasure at all above the earth,

and a longing takes hold of me for death
and to see the river Acheron
with its banks of lotus flowers wet with dew.'

1

As Richard's field, like a tile slipping
on a pitched roof, keeps in spite of the heave-
and-heft of the underearth a tilted equilibrium;

so I, down the hill in a sloping-
up house with a slipping-down garden, try to achieve
a steadier state without benefit of Librium;

as Chris in this locality celebrates his *vacherin
Mont d'or* cheese with a musical quodlibet
of ayres and graces from greater times;

so sing, goddess, since a little Acheron
is running below Holme like a final couplet,
sing of our great goings-on in greater terms.

Variations on Sappho 95

2

The walnut kernels
I'm adding to our pasta as a garnish,
with their matching hemispheres, fissures, fosses and canals,
are brains
from the six-inch manikins that walked all over Gulliver,
that tied him down with ribbons
or ribands of obligation.

Our cat himself comes in, William,
and obliges me with yet another coercive homunculus, live
and dangling from his mouth by a limb.

3

Someone will approach you and sit down
on this very bench, Chris, you've wired with headphones
for hearing the *Goldbergs* or what you please ('Observe those conifers,
their plantation observes the golden ratio'),

as sometimes you yourself sat down
by Patrick Kavanagh, observer on that lotus-bank of the Dublin
    Grand Canal,
on his very lotus-bench by a lock ('This channel
falls from Lake Erie into Lake Ontario');

someone will approach you and set down
this: 'Hoard the past as capital for poems, or allow it
to go running away like watery verse,
or see in it what you set down
as divine proportion (or what you please). We will wait
on this very bench, observe and converse.'

Variations on Sappho 95

4

Your loft ladder, Chris, is a climbing wall,
a plank from skirting to ceiling
with holes for rungs, the easiest climb of all
that you did from the Alps to the Cuillins.

The black humour's
on you, though your shelves of climbing-guides one above the
  other
rise like ridges, though you can see to Holme Moss
with its transmitter mast like a ladder above the earth.

5

Hokusai-san, the breaking wave
of snow I fell in
under banks of snow, *seppi*, on Watery Lane

holds me here like a boat held off from land,
from all England.
I choose not to wave.

Variations on Sappho 95

6

A sound of bedsprings or a huge divan
rhythmically complaining,
came from outside, from ground
at the back, at midnight. Troubled, I got up to the window.

In the dark were our neighbours Tim and Vanda
trampolining
high above the earth in their garden,
where the holly hedge was already wet with dew.

They divine
already from the plethora of berries, what a matter of moment
it is, while they are
as they are, flesh and vein,
to take pleasure above the earth, from the movement
of the body itself through the air.

7

Linked under a single big umbrella
that was singing from the rain,
Tina and Rod on our doorstep hand over
an invitation. They'd stepped from that Renoir
painting of umbrellas, or were hand-in-hand under
a *parapluie de Cherbourg*. I was vague
as a lotus-eater about accepting. In spite of my social failure
they ran off with a wave, *la nouvelle vague*.

8

Linked in a single long take
Jacqueline and I are seen
by anyone passing our uncurtained kitchen windows
in a neo-realist mise-en-scène,
discussing at the cooker whether it is the new Wim Wenders
that we must see. Think this plotless scene,
for the moment you took
to see it, part of the hermetic grand design.

9

Look, cattle by Cuyp
have entered the frame of our picture window, our frame
of reference, as I entered their
gilded frame in the National Gallery.

Engage them, Ms Dally,
in conversation, feed them with grasses, keep them here,
gilded cattle from
some ideal riverbank, detain them with buttercups.

As Richard's field is depressed
by the weight of their certainty, their gold-plated
positive certitude, though they stand propped on stick-
legs like cattleboats on the stocks,
we know that like gold they will have departed
before we've got their cud-like convictions appraised.

Variations on Sappho 95

10

My lord, I'm not for winter, and wait it out
holed up like a monk in a land that's sinned
in an empty age. These woods were stripped
for punishment, their leaves have bled downwind.

The anchoress of Shere for some 'nefarious
committed sin' is immured in a church nook,
squinnying at a squint-hole. Holy fires
illuminate heretics from the Holy Book.

11

I've turned the sinless pages of the *Summa*
as God might turn me, as in Aquino
itself some creature now perfected, late
in the evening, might turn its ox-like head.

I sit high-backed under a baldacchino
of broad-leaved trees (each one a cowl or hood
of thought), on a landscaped lawn, in summer
in England, under the great cone of light.

Variations on Sappho 95

12

A steely cattlegrid bars the drive
at Bill and Jean's. Do they expect a drove
of shambling cattle, an influx
of all kinds of kine from Aberdeen Angus to zebu?
Are this gridiron and pit a barbie
of heroic proportions, for Hermes to roast an unlawful ox?
Or an oubliette for the life I ruined, kaputt,
the things I'd rather drop and forget like cowpats?

'Admit us gilded cattle by Cuyp, let us come in
at your boundary stones or herms,
divinely proportioned in ourselves,
such vessels
of weighty affirmation, let us commune
with you, in spite of his cynical humours.'

13

Now Robert's cattle eeeeease
through slip-in gaps in the walls and palings
into Richard's Elysian leaze or field, easing themselves
of all that's pressing on them as they pass.

And I slip slipshod down through all the levels
of the sloping-
off house and garden, to find some piece of the self, some peace
of a slip of a self, that consistently is.

14

Risen from the foam
of the shower-
gel, I brush out the coil
of my golden hair,
this mortal coil.
In the mirror
I'm glum
enough for Venus
come on a scallop-shell
which zephyrs did propel
to this island of sandy
Cyprus,
sand
and sad cypress.

15

The grand Steinway
which I was never allowed to play
migrated with us. I watched them haul
father's precious crateful
of Beethoven
higher and higher at Bellapaix
to our high *piano nobile*. His eleven
good companions
pushed, pulled, pulleyed and manhandled
that sarcoffergus of Bachs
the shape of Cyprus itself with its panhandle.
Our migration was a cross between Laurel
and Hardy's music box,
and Jane Campion's.

Variations on Sappho 95

16

Look down from the *piano nobile*
as if from the upper circle
of an Odeon
or the tiers of an ancient odeion
('a theatre for musical
competitions', though I'm the mere custodian
of the noble piano),
look down, Clodiana,
as if from the quarterdeck of an old-world
P&O
or a top bunk
or berth, or the brink
of a lotus-bank
to the soulful underworld.

17

Pumped up like quadriceps or thighs
the hills on the horizon
are a zone
of the high goddess who flexes her thews
over me. Though I'd run
upstairs to the ninth or nineteenth
attic and jump in the air from the plinth
of a sloping ridgetile, though I reach
the height of anxiety,
I do not reach her blest society,
not even to her toenail
though I stretch
my neck like Alice's drawn
by Tenniel.

Variations on Sappho 95

18

Risen in resin from the foam
in my fish-
pond, statuesque, is a copy
of a copy
of a copy
of an antique female form.
As the pond and garden conform, Clodiana,
to the golden
ratio, as the water circles
and the golden rational fish calculate
their cycles
as they circulate,
let us figure how the selfish
mind may no longer circle itself.

19

The ancient Greek poets
conversed in epithets
like Agamemnon the callous phallus
or Helen with the rosy, fingered breasts.

20

Helen's own daughter, I think, could not compare
with you when I see you face to face. You
are such as Helen herself with the golden hair,

white-armed, at a parapet wall with a view,
not Troy's but a radar post or lookout,
unmanned at peace on Lesbos. As you review

waves of the Aegean from this new outlook,
new Helen, I watch your strawberry-yellow hair
and something else to which we both look out.

21

No wonder, Ms Dally,
the florist mistook your name for Mrs Dalloway

when you gathered sickle arm-
fuls of arum-

lilies, irises, delphiniums and lilac,
all that we've come to lack

since the flowering of modernism … Stand,
as an urn and vase shall always stand

on your étagère and music cabinet
or a kitchen unit,

over-
flowering with flowers and with greenery leafed over

Variations on Sappho 95

to the leaf everlasting. Never endue
the sickly lotuses with their due.

22

The preacher put down his Jesuitical biretta
regretfully on the pulpit shelf
like Bond in '58 putting aside his Beretta,

and produced from an inner pocket or sleeve
as if from inside himself
some sermon notes on what we might believe.

I believe in one God, the Father who might be.
I believe in none god, i'faith not a moiety.
I believe in the goddesses, fair and far, that we might be.

23

Ken found at the top of Olympus
which he climbed in a tweed jacket like Edward Whymper's
a goddess
in a soft bustle gown with a princess bodice.

24

On the other hand it may be Thetis
you spoke to, Ken,
sylphy
sea-self
more tidal than orthography
itself, who refused you her autograph
or any such token,
whose thisness may have been that of Themisto or Tethys.

'You think of the self,' she said, 'as a thatness,
as if you were proper nouns
substantive, who overbear
to be. O human modal particles, O you whose whatness
is that of indefinite pronouns,
you're dependent on the action of a greater verb.'

25

This compost bin embodies the golden ratio.
Graham's squared-off
timbers stand four-square
in a rectangle
among the curvaceous borders. The body of worms
warms
to its earthy task. They're rejoicing that the longer
side of their soft mansion
is equal to the square root of five minus one
over two, that divine proportion.

Variations on Sappho 95

We'll haul our bodies like a cablecar
up Middleton Fell, as high as they've been
above the wormy earth.
Vitruvian bin,
grant as our eternal pastime some 'truly remarkable
proof' of Fermat's last theorem.

26

Here I began, precipitated like dew
from the moon (I'm told by the wise centaur Karen)
or risen as if from death
autochthonous on this bank or bench of earth.
It cannot be true
I belonged somewhere else, as the poet of origins said.

Whatever my poem, a mere poem, said,
it may not be true
that I lay on the earth
like a lotus and hoped for a decorous death,
though someone I loved may have been carried off like carrion
by Kieron the ferryman, or by Eros like the faithless dew.

27

Hermes himself came in looking for argument.
'My lady, your ninetyfifth fragment

(as it shall be) ends
with decorous dewy-eyed lotuses – schmotuses, a self-indulgence

that will blight poets
(those sighing generations) like crops of potatoes.

Lady S, you're slipping
as the sloping house itself is schlepping,

downhill.' 'Schlemiel! Though I'm on this local lotus-bank
or bench of earth, on this very bench

of time, my songs or artefacts,
whose certitude is greater than any statement of the facts,

stand
detached from us, as an urn or vase shall always stand.'

Variations on Sappho 95

28

Polyphilophloisboisterous
the waves along our human strand,
kinder than humans, shall efface
these acts cut in its flesh or sand.

And Tzetzes, tetchy polymath
Byzantine, tells how Sappho's rhyme,
lyre, songs and singer, have become
contingent casualties of time.

29

Though your apron's printed all over with slimy-lime-green figures
of frogs
I decline to transform you with a kiss,
princess already to the very bodice.

30

Since I would be Jacqui's suitor,
Hermes, herdsman, be my escort
past her cattle gilt and hirsute.

Hermes Hermes
harum-scarum
horum harum
do not harm us

Since I would be Jacqui's lover,
look, her sickle arms like lilies
reach among the modern lilacs.

Hermes Hermes
shammer scammer
'llorum 'llarum
have good humours

Jacqui, which ones are verbenas,
which verbascums, which viburnums,
since I cannot tell between us.

Hermes Hermes
herm and harem
quorum quarum
home us holme us

31

Hermes himself came in. I said,
'By the blessed goddess, let it be believed
what Sappho, goddess now, in garlands tells us,

though we will end like lotuses, lettuces
brainless on a bank of Acheron,
we too were goddesses when we were loved.'

III

First Letter to Ed

Awaking one's lute, Ed, goes back to a psalm:
    in the Prayer Book David
with a lute sings praise in adversity. We're less divided;
let us praise Thomas Wyatt and sing harm
    to adversaries and animadverters. When we're devoid
of comfort, wake up, lutes, no longer keep
    your late, loutish sleep.

All things averse to me, all animus and afflictions
    (though with his lute George Herbert
sings that by such our sinful nature's inhibited),
all these harm me only, with melancholy fluxions
    and malignant humours. I inhabit
a malcontented spot, with lute songs on a shelf
    but nothing of myself.

I admire, Ed, those who are whole, of a piece,
    like Herbert's country parson,
sin-carrier, priggish, but altogether his own person
(well, his dear God's). Grant us thy peace.
    We in adversity have personae
in verse: you've been Hakagawa and a Scottish Sufi,
    I am anticke Sappho.

Somewhere there must be a suitable image of Sappho
    with a lute, a fairer Wyatt
in travesty. If we are whatever we make, whatever
we fabricate from the diverse perverse reverses we suffer,
    we know what we're for.
Poetry is making something, Sappho's *poiesis*,
    and we've made a couple of pieces.

First Letter to Ed

All our inverse outcomes, all the animosity
    of the cosmos, were never the converse
of the self. Whenever our dissolute lutes converse,
without Herbert's priestly habit of theodicy,
    and disparage this disappointing universe,
we conserve the self. What counts, Ed, is the fact
    that, better or worse, we act.

Awaking Jacqui, her body like a lute, from sleep,
    or talking with you as far
as we walk in a day, and learning of another as fair,
I'm held in a community, as Little Gidding would keep
    and comfort Nicholas Ferrar.
Each night they'd read between them, as if linking arms,
    the complete cycle of the Psalms.

Second Letter to Ed

    The complete cycle of the Psalms
illumined most what was dark in him, Milton would assert
when his reader read to him, or when he'd state, restate
and counterstate a defence of the Commonwealth in arms,
        the state dictating. Your letter
from Bradford, Ed, unveils a mere velleity,
to inquire along Leeds Road what it is that avails
        in a synagogue, church or mosque,
in a chapel or temple. O Leeds Road is a masque
in scene after scene, Leeds Road is our earthly vale.

    You live, Ed, in attics
which the urban trees reach for. Their leaves aspire
to the printed leaves and quires and sheaves of papers
that live with you. To you I send my letters to Atticus,
        and ask, is there a value
in the spirit of place, does a *deus loci* avail you?
While I live in Holme in a version of pastoral I imagine
        all Arcadia here,
on a local moor in a little locality; but here
there'll still be alteration in things, and things to mourn in elegy.

    On the local moor a boardwalk,
built on stilts on a boggy succulent section
of the footpath, carries me over the sogs and suction
as the present over the past. I walk abroad,
        but the past is frogs and polliwogs
under the boardwalk. I determine, Ed, as a wag
of determinism, I'm just a mime of my foredoings to now,
        a meme of others'. Expel
the wretched ineradicable past. My present principle
is uncertainty: am I waveform, locus or merely momentum now?

Second Letter to Ed

      I live, Ed, in attics
as high as Milton's prose style. High leaves,
which seem the aspiring nature of their trees, are veils
for their failures. I write to you because in Attica
      something once lived
which might in our time, I thought, be again revealed.
Below me someone is calling aloud and dying.
      Someone else lives,
in a little Arcadia in a masque, for whom something avails.
None of this, of course, is God's or my own or anyone's doing.

Third Letter to Ed

    My own or anyone's doing,
casuists tell us, explains nothing enough;
more complex explications (but with a but or an if),
       historical inevitabilities and sociological causes,
must be pondered, Ed, like Ciceronian dependent clauses.
But nothing explains enough old age undoing
       the person. I'd thought each person
one, an integration, all of a piece, one peace,
two existences, body and other, like lovers;
but they leave one another, whatever that other is, both master-leavers.

       I see us dead. The young
with limbs like lumbering logs of flesh, their infants
made flesh among us, Ed, those fat infantas –
       I see them dead, hollowed out
like log canoes, to be borne at shoulder height,
hulls and hullings, holes. Even as we're breathing,
       the body like a cadence aspires
to its end; its last words are, Nothing shall spare us.
So now new values avail us; our fiction
is fact, transient permanent, separation union, imperfect perfection.

       We live, merely human,
on a local moor holme-like, an isle without magicks,
a seabank of reason. We've knowledge of the major works
       of Shakespeare. If our time, Ed, is a sentence,
a Ciceronian period, we stay in the present tense.
We live wholly human, all too human,
       converse like gods, settle
like social animals on our soil (log-house, log-settle).
Here we complete or piece ourselves; each does,
each one; each pair of lovers is two-in-one; so nothing shall undo us.

The Left Arm

Apple-shaped John, John-apple, apple
corps and corpus, found
things fall apart, the cincture cannot hold
all that he was, all that his waist confined.

Ken was bent double or triple
by backpain, from climbing the bookstacks
of his private library of Alexandria, whose latest holdings
nest on the tops like storks.

Your own left arm, Jacqueline mavourneen,
has been surgically opened and resealed
with a part cut out like a censored letter, mavrone.

As you cannot carry a shield
I'll shield you as best I can when you fight, as you will,
at Stirling Bridge and Bannockburn and with the O'Neill.

Your Body Undressed

Your body undressed
this night sky is, of white stars,
light itself undressed.

In Sicyon

1

In spite of the cucumber
you wept like Crashaw's weeper from an allergy or hay-
fever, as you lay
in Sicyon like one laid out, with seagreen
slices for pennies on your eyes.
At supper you wept over the seabream,
garnished though it was with sea cucumber.

2

Thanks to her cucumbers
Praxilla
was derided by the scholiasts and scholars for being silly,
when she made the mournful
Adonis say as he lay like a coin in Hades,
what he missed the most, after the sunlight and full moon,
was ripe apples, pears and cucumbers.

Narcissus Poeticus

Hosts of golden daffodils,
we host crowds of you, our rooms
are guestrooms for your communal vases. We are most affable,
we gratify your narcissism
and regale you with tapwater, O yellow affodills.

Your initial *d*
conferred on a whim by the Tudors, has never been explained
to the satisfaction of the *OED*,
no more than I could explain
what he does or why, or she or I, or John Doe or John Dee.

Affodowndaffodowndillies, we bear you home like fardels
heavy with knowledge
of your own, something ineffable.
Come share the half-guessed rooms we lodge in,
you who used to be asphodels.

Grass

The grass anticipates the cows,
spires and aspires
upwards like an aspirational consumer society,
to be consumed.

No. It is the grassfed wisdom
of the cows, their sobriety
in judgment, for which the grass suspires.
Cows do not say, 'It is the cause, it is the cause.'

'No,' the aspirant grasses say, and aspirate
each word, 'it is the kind forbearance
of kine, themselves an image … '

I am greener than grass and imagine
how once before
I aspired to love or sufferance or something in that spirit.

Cattle Console Him

1

    Cattle of consolation,
come down, cattle goddesses of five hundred kilos,
sundisk bodies, bellies, digesters of cellulose,
    come down to my anxious field.
    Once before you filed
into the frame of our picture window, ate our windbreak
of Cupressocyparis leylandii, spoke, and broke wind.
    Come to me now, tell me the solution,
why it's here or there that a cow occurs
in a random field, why you're moved without cause.

2

    Boethius in his prison
saw no cause for the headfirst destruction he would suffer
or the king's Gothic cruelties, until Philosophy
    herself came below
    and nudged his writing elbow:
'Give up your headwork, reasoning and knowledge, Boethius.
It's divine providence.' Let her not console us both
    with a gift grown upon misprision.
You thought you were one of the Sun's sun-gilded cattle,
but he sold you off to death, less good than chattel.

Cattle Console Him

3

    Thomas in his cell,
a monastic cell in Windesheim, who seems to imitate
not Christ but all experience, counsellor and intimate –
    you know how sharply I'm aggrieved
    by the shortcomings of others, how grieved
that my own happiness comes short. Though I will not seek
dead Christ pinned out like a cattle skin,
    how much, Thomas, your book consoles us.
He endured great trials, says the *Chronicle*. He was buried
in the east cloister, by the side of Peter Hebort.

4

    The cattle console me.
We are no manger moocows who bend the knee
at midnight, but hardier. Like us, be here and now,
    mired in the flesh hocks-
    and-oxters. Turn ox-
wise at the end of every furrow, pull the oxharrow
of your human nature. O her hair is oxlip-yellow,
    her body curved like a meadowgrass, a culm
of grassflowers. Love her, like herself, whatever occurs,
be moved as cattle are moved, love without cause.

These Cattle

These are the cattle of Holme. These cattle
come on at a trot, kick their heels,

kick their helm or hovel
head over heels,

kick over the gates and pales and rails
and take to their heels

down the village street, helter-
skelter, heel and toe, showing their heels.

May they never be turned or caught, or haltered
or tied by the heels.

But one day Hermes of Holme
with his wand as light as a grass stem or haulm

will escort them home,
back to Far End, between the gate-wards or herms

of Rake Lane,
still at a run or rake, in a line,

down the narrow rake or clough, downhill
with a god at their heels,

to the grass-culmy isles
of the blessed, where they may cool their heels.

Reaching Chios

I run on a watery track through Holme Woods,
through birch, oak and conifers, and holly or holm woods,

on a track improved by the reservoir contractors
to a heaving seaway for their dozers and Caterpillar tractors;

I run past Jim Howard's black cattle on Netherley
unwinding surly and sorrowly over the lea;

I run on, to Ramsden Reservoir, a black sea.
Cleisthenes, death caught up with you on the Black Sea

wandering. Buried in foreign ground,
you missed the sweet returning home that's honey to the mind.

Whomever on the sea tracks I call to mind,
we do not reach Chios with the sea running round.

Groundsel

I am at the door-sill, the ground-sill, the very groundsel-edge
of old age.

Age-old Greeks,
already in waiting to be shades of Hades, already geeks

of their own language and intellect, were the first to make this
    metaphor.
What they meant it for

was not the initial going in
to the anteroom which is old age, but leaving again.

*

Common groundsel, Senecio vulgaris, with its seedhead
like an old knight whitehaired,

was used in poultices for toothache or an abscess.
There's no old remedy for absence,

or leaving. At this doorway I've no more to do.
Let me go through.

For a Wedding

Enter the Greek sea, for it sends toward you
its white-armed goddess-waves,
which cherish their beach like seagoddess-wives.

Graves, as an old Apollo by the sea at Deya,
a myth of himself, ordains
that a true poem invoke his White Goddess, the Muse,
by whom, my lady, he is undone.

His offwhite muses – mistress or miss,
mare or Mary, but never to marry – he courts
with *fin'amors* subserviently. They leave him, without a curtsy.

Enter the Greek sea, for it sends the seamews,
the ungodly gulls, toward us. Seawoman,
muse but no deity, today
let us marry, though we whiten here like the sea, all-human.

IV

Holme

1

    We come in consort,
Jacqui and Chris, Mary and Ken, Jean
and Bill, to hear ayres and fancies, a concert
    of madrigals apt for voyce and viols.
    We come to hear *Susanne un jour*
'full sad & sore molested'; we hope for elegies
and lovesick nymphs and neatherds. In our own ill usage
such pleasaunt songes and sweet invention certes shall avail us.

    We come from Holme,
that small Parnassus, where we converse in counterpoint
point against point, where cattle console us in their helm.
    Those makers of music come, in veils,
    whom death releases to us, unpent
to play here, Gibbons and Byrd, Lassus and Lawes.
Sit at your music-desks, no longer strengthless.
Before we are shades, make us for this time your voice and viols.

2

Ken is walking on Netherley moor in blank
    snow: no snow
clinquant like coin which makes the image of Xmas,
    where X marks
    a spot of time redemptive: snow
that's nowhere, snow where he blinks against the iceblink.
    He limps, with one arm and one leg too
longer than the other, from a burden he cannot let go.

Nothing's here: not a soul, though there never were
    any such: no
sole or solitary other: not even a self,
    so no false
    self either. Redemptive snow
has covered his tracks, all there ever were
    from the beginning. Ken has been and gone
in the no of snow. Let him begin again.

3

Bright Cecilia
hails from a heaven as high as her own high C,
descends
her scale-stairs, and condescends
to Jean's summer party in Holme. Her connection with music is
    putative,
but she carries her organetto, her portative
organ slung on her shoulder. See
how all art, she sings, aspires to the condition of Purcell.

She moves *cantabile* among the summery guests,
these bright populations. I follow her *lentamente*,
listening. They have not guessed
how much I cherish my own anxieties, how much I lament
already
the sorrows and separation for which I am not ready.

*

Leonardo's Cecilia
is staying the week at Jean's. The winter is as chilly

as her disposition. Her pet stoat is ermined
as if it could even redeem her

with its snowy coat. 'However great thou art,'
says the painted one to the sainted other, 'great art

is not abstract but human.' I am moved to tell her of the ancient
actor who mispronounced an accent

in Greek, so the audience heard that mad Orestes,
after his storming, was again, again restored

to a stoat of calm.
Ha. Again, again I have come

to social grief. I leave her, and join
those who stand at a different portrait, Stubley's Jean.

*

Paul Simon's Cecilia
has left him again, herself as withey and sallowy

as Jean's water garden in spring. Let us do as Pound,
remake our history. She looks at the pond,

which is also reflective. An old pond. Water jumps kerplog
into the sound of a frog.

Couzen frog, I might have supposed
that everything I do and suffer is a shapely purposed

progress: I, Persephone,
ascend from the dead and dayligone to the day's epiphany,

reaching the light. Goddess of shades, undo
my uncaused unkindness and whatever I've misdone,

all my sad encounters.
Art is the best of what we did, those songs and cantos.

*

Holme

Italianato Cecil
(speak him with the long E M Forster used)
is obliged to visit his country cousins. He mourns and moons
in Jean's autumnal garden
sere-leaved. O a woman like a Leonardo
has abandoned him, sore left. He could never tell what she
    means.
He opens Dante. An aesthete ill-used,
the great books are with him, though love will cease.

No, no – tell him, Jacqui, hare
of the brown moon – tell him, each of us is an art-
work most artful, and love is the art-
like value in us. Jacqui, there's brown hair
on your long, furlong ears. Let it cure their itchy eczema
and everything, O my hare love, that's irksome.

4

That day, Susanna, when the two old men
sex would exact, who used to covet
your beauty, you were grieved without comfort
by the efforts they made for your own demesne.
You told them, 'If I choose dishonesty
and give you joy and joyaunce of my body,
it's all up with me. If I've not obeyed you,
you'll have me put to death, as much dishonoured.
I'll rather suffer in innocence,
than sin and do my Seigneur an offence.'

Holme

5

He would have pursued the beck up Watery Lane,
its bed as difficult as any in which he'd lain,
but the sunken trackway's heavy growth
of bushes, brush, undergrowth and overgrowth
stopped him. The trees hung down like lop-ears. Besides,
he had grown heavy himself, a lopsided
Lob of the countryside. The lane not taken,
that lane, he thought, must be the one I took
loping lightfoot once when I chose it. It has led
here, after all, where we have settled
by the fields at Far End. Here we belong
as briefly as the harebells and as long.

Holme

6

Ken has erected on their social lawn
polyester gazebos and marquees
of air and landscape. Here Mary de Staël holds her salon.
We circulate like marquises and *marquises*.
A salmon from the salmon-crowded farms
has come on a dish to feed us.
Salmon of knowledge, confide to us
how you lie here, *nature morte*, with such a sense of form.

'Whole skyfuls of blue delphiniums
have been cut off
and stand on Mary's terrace in water-jars. Delphi is a name
for knowledge which I cannot now put off,
about the world. I had aspired
to be some local
fixture, a landform or feature, hummock- or holm-like,
but our knowledge unpieces me; I am everywhere dispersed.'

'Petals of the sawn-off delphiniums
patter like offcuts
of sky onto the terrace floor. Socialism
we affected, because she like a lover affects us.
She might have been the form of the century past.
I have seen comrade Lenin in his underworld
waxen and waning. I willed
his consul shade to counsel us, but they made me hurry past.'

Holme

'I know delphiniums
come from the Greek for a dolphin. Those dolphin-crowded seas
formed such images. Capitalism
is Dead Seas.
On Bishopsgate and Old Broad Street, Canary Wharf and St Mary
    Axe
the towers of finance
aspire like instruments of debt and credit in their fineness.
Whatever is humane has limits, says Marcus Aurelius, or Marx.'

The salmon of the west is caught and slain,
for all his knowledge. The salon philosophers queue
to eat the wisdom of Salomon and Solon.
It is late to rescue
those who die like cut delphiniums
at some new Troy, the poor who are offered
only a usury they cannot afford,
and all who are unregarded, hardly names or forms.

7

Ken is holding the van's open tailgate
on his shoulders, the hatch of the hatchback
on his Atlantean back,
as the mechanism has failed. Below this metal sky

Mary is to and fro the van, and under his tall gate
conveys her puppets and marionettes, shadow-
puppets of themselves, whom she stows as shades
in the dim interior. Ken holds up the mortal sky.

Holme

8

We come from Holme to Notre-Dame, taller
than its tall tales of God. Shades of the dead
are waiting for us, veiled in voile and tulle,
Vierne and Widor and Duruflé, whom Persephone undid
to play for us. Their organ notes rise up like loaded
pillars to the vaulting windows. The living
shall be considered with the dead, all whom we love.

*

Saint Jean opens a window in Erquy.
It frames in a kindly frame
red houses, red gardens, red boats, a red quay,
red people. The human forms
are outlines, mere outer line, which a red ground informs.
They may be happier so. By the window there's a reproduction,
Dufy's 'Open window at St-Jeannet'.

Bill runs and runs on the sands at Cap d'Erquy towing
young Anne like a cockboat. The high cape
diminishes them. Irruptive irritable waves are toing and froing,
interruptions the sand cannot escape.
The even sandscape
has conferred on Bill its own forbearance. Nymphs and undines
of the sea have not undone him.

Pétoncles, palourdes, huîtres, moules, étrilles, coquilles Saint-Jacques,
maquereau, morue, blennie, lieu jaune,
whatever the sea gives up shall be devoured. Sainte-Jacqui
and Jean, at their Roman lunch

Holme

as the western empire declines, such learned
diners, they shall become, in some greater encyclopedia or
 catalogue,
a list of the seafood of Gaul.

Having divided Gaul into three parts
Mary and Ken drive on, to the northern marches and the border
 legions,
to sing with the children of Romania. Their puppets
emerge from the van with Persephone. They play the legend
of the Winter King and the Summer Queen, by a rainbow conjoined.
The king and queen dance each year round,
the dead of Europe go under the ground.

Mary unveils a lifesize picture of a legionary, *miles*;
like Ken in costume, he steps from the frame
across its boundary or *limes*.
Roman, romance, roman de geste, Roumi, Romaic or Rom,
come stand beside us in this anteroom.
The king and queen dance each of us round,
the dead of Europe come up from the ground.

*

They came from Holme, those singers of tales,
those seaside runners and epicureans. What they did
I have told. And of Jacqui too my hare love I tell,
O brown hare sandy-haired,
how she it was in Notre-Dame, as the organ sounded,
though I would leave, though all we have will leave us,
she it was sat down among the living.

A Note About the Author

Chris Preddle has retired to a windy shoulder of the Pennines in West Yorkshire. Born in London in 1943, he was educated in South Africa and at Stonyhurst College in Lancashire, where he was taught by Peter Levi. He read Medieval and Modern Greek at the University of Oxford. He worked in public libraries in London, Elgin and Kendal, and as a librarian for two child care charities, Barnardo's and Action for Children. He compiled a revised edition of the leading library classification of social welfare, the Bliss Bibliographic Classification (Class Q). He is married to Jacqui, and they have four grownup children between them and two grandchildren. His first collection was *Bonobos* (Newcastle upon Tyne: Biscuit Publishing, 2001). He is presently working on English versions of all Sappho's poems and fragments.

Other books from Waywiser

POETRY

Al Alvarez, *New & Selected Poems*
Robert Conquest: *Penultimata*
Morri Creech, *Field Knowledge*
Peter Dale, *One Another*
Erica Dawson, *Big-Eyed Afraid*
B. H. Fairchild, *The Art of the Lathe*
Jeffrey Harrison, *The Names of Things: New & Selected Poems*
Joseph Harrison, *Identity Theft*
Joseph Harrison, *Someone Else's Name*
Anthony Hecht, *Collected Later Poems*
Anthony Hecht, *The Darkness and the Light*
Carrie Jerrell, *After the Revival*
Rose Kelleher, *Bundle o' Tinder*
Dora Malech, *Shore Ordered Ocean*
Eric McHenry, *Potscrubber Lullabies*
Timothy Murphy, *Very Far North*
Ian Parks, *Shell Island*
Daniel Rifenburgh, *Advent*
W.D. Snodgrass: *Not for Specialists: New & Selected Poems**
Mark Strand, *Blizzard of One**
Bradford Gray Telford: *Perfect Hurt*
Cody Walker, *Shuffle and Breakdown*
Deborah Warren, *The Size of Happiness*
Clive Watkins, *Jigsaw*
Richard Wilbur, *Mayflies**
Richard Wilbur, *Collected Poems 1943-2004*
Norman Williams, *One Unblinking Eye*
Greg Williamson, *A Most Marvelous Piece of Luck*

FICTION

Gregory Heath, *The Entire Animal*
Matthew Yorke, *Chancing It*

ILLUSTRATED

Nicholas Garland, *I wish ...*

NON-FICTION

Neil Berry, *Articles of Faith: The Story of British Intellectual Journalism*
Mark Ford, *A Driftwood Altar: Essays and Reviews*
Richard Wollheim, *Germs: A Memoir of Childhood*

*Expanded UK edition